CITIZEN SCIENCE PROJECTS

Invasive Species Projects

BY CHRISTA KELLY

Kids Core

An Imprint of Abdo Publishing
abdobooks.com

abdobooks.com

Printed in the United States of America, North Mankato, Minnesota.
102025
012026

Cover Photo: Shutterstock Images
Interior Photos: Randy Runtsch/Shutterstock Images, 4–5; Irina Kozorog/Shutterstock Images, 7; Rostislav Stefanek/Shutterstock Images, 9; Edvard Ellric/Shutterstock Images, 10 (top left); Jay Ondreicka/Shutterstock Images, 10 (top right); Shutterstock Images, 10 (bottom left), 16, 18, 26, 29 (top); Vicky Wiedira/Shutterstock Images, 10 (bottom right); Dennis Molenaar/Shutterstock Images, 12–13; Sandra Burm/Shutterstock Images, 15; Lasse Johansson/Shutterstock Images, 20–21; Oksana Akhtanina/Shutterstock Images, 23; Maxal Tamor/Shutterstock Images, 25; Ekkasit A. Siam/Shutterstock Images, 28 (top); Pornpimon Ainkaew/Shutterstock Images, 28 (bottom); Anna Gratys/Shutterstock Images, 29 (bottom)

Editor: Trudy Becker
Series Designer: Marley Richmond

Library of Congress Control Number: 2025939875

Publisher's Cataloging-in-Publication Data

Names: Kelly, Christa, author.
Title: Invasive species projects / by Christa Kelly
Description: Minneapolis, Minnesota: Abdo Publishing, 2026 | Series: Citizen science projects | Includes online resources and index.
Identifiers: ISBN 9781098298579 (lib. bdg.) | ISBN 9798384932376 (ebook)
Subjects: LCSH: Science projects--Juvenile literature. | Field experiments--Juvenile literature. | Introduced organisms--Juvenile literature. | Foreign species (Introduced organisms)--Juvenile literature. | Balance of nature--Juvenile literature. | Ecology--Experiments--Juvenile literature. | Ecological science--Juvenile literature.
Classification: DDC 507.8--dc23

CONTENTS

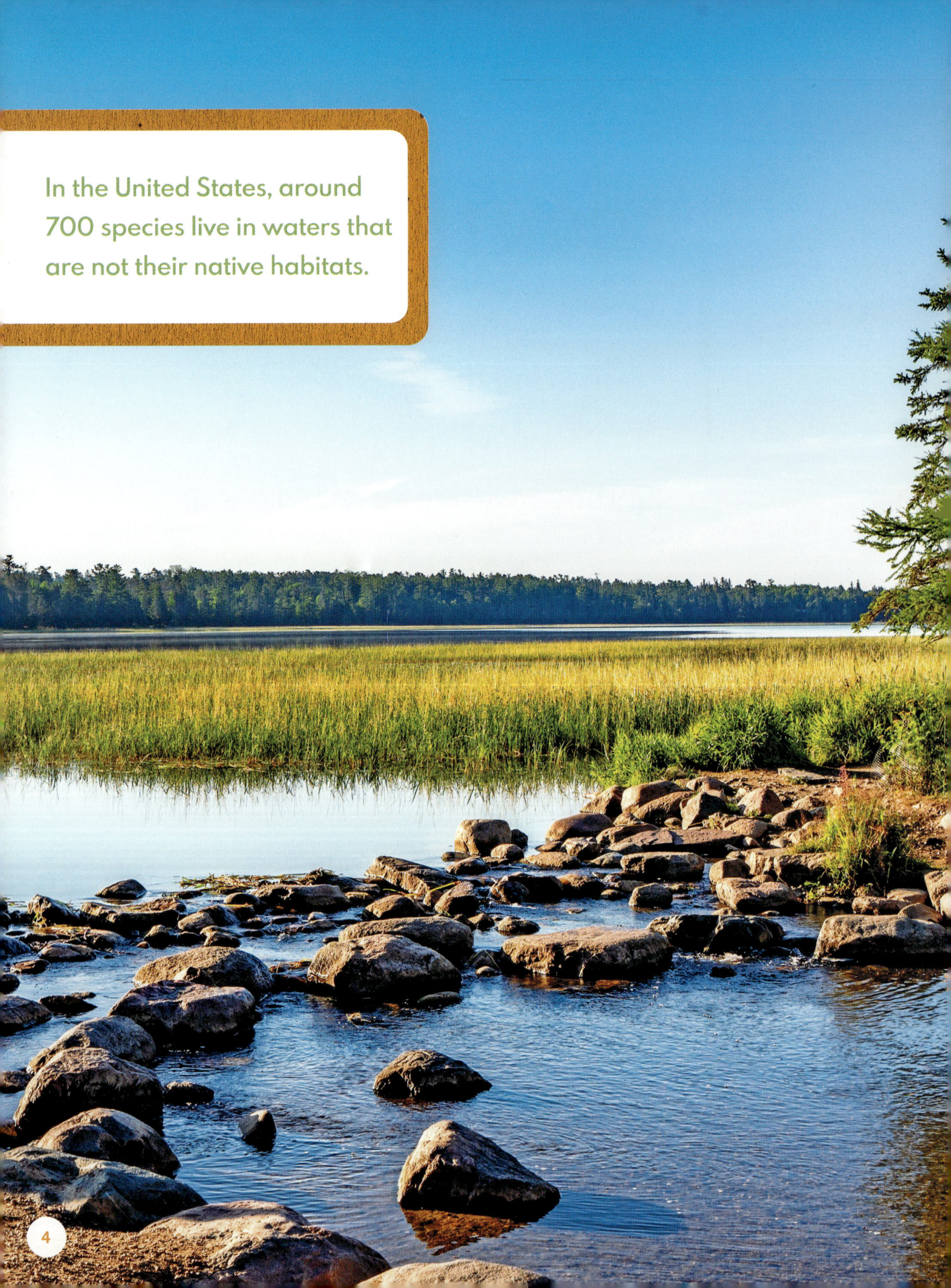

In the United States, around 700 species live in waters that are not their native habitats.

CHAPTER 1

Saving the River

Maisie and her friends carefully walked down the slippery riverbank. Their class was on a field trip. The students came to collect **data** about the animals in the river.

Maisie's teacher had taught the class about invasive **species**.

These plants and animals move into a new area. Then they start to take over. They hurt the **ecosystem**. Maisie's class wanted to help. So she and her classmates joined a program called FishTracker. People can use it to track invasive species. Maisie's class needed to check the river.

Maisie put on a rubber glove. Then she dipped a clean water bottle into the river.

Why Are Invasive Species Bad?

Invasive species often harm native species. For example, invasive plants may block sunlight from reaching other plants. Invasive animals may eat native animals. Or they may take food that native animals need. That can put the ecosystem out of balance.

Some data collection projects require glass containers. Others may allow plastic materials.

She filled up the bottle. Next, Maisie poured the water through a filter. The filter would capture environmental DNA (eDNA). That is the **genetic material** living things leave behind. Her friend used tweezers to place the filter into a test tube.

At the end of the day, the teacher gathered all the samples. She sent them to the scientists that run FishTracker. They would collect eDNA from the filter. Then they could study the eDNA to learn which species are in an area.

A few weeks later, the results arrived. The eDNA showed that an invasive fish species lived in the river. It was the round goby. This fish eats the eggs of native fish. Now scientists knew about the problem. They could work to fix it. Maisie was proud. Her class had helped protect the river.

Citizen Science

Citizen scientists are regular people who help scientists do research. People all over the world

The round goby is native to Europe. It first arrived in US waters in 1990.

take part in citizen science projects. These projects gather lots of data. Then scientists use the data in their studies.

Invasive Species in North America

Asian carp

Native to China

Invasive in the Great Lakes and Mississippi River basin

Zebra mussels

Native to eastern Europe and western Russia

Invasive in the Great Lakes and northern United States

Purple loosestrife

Native to Europe and Asia

Invasive across the United States and Canada

Emerald ash borer

Native to northeastern Asia

Invasive in the eastern and midwestern United States and Canada

Invasive species can cause harm to native environments, plants, and animals.

Some citizen scientists help prevent the spread of invasive species. They join programs such as FishTracker. In some projects, people record invasive species that they see. In others, people help remove invasive species. These citizen scientists can help protect the ecosystems around them.

Further Evidence

Look at the webpage below. Does it give any new evidence to support Chapter One?

Invasive Species

abdocorelibrary.com/invasive-species-projects

Nutria are invasive in many US states. People are encouraged to report sightings.

Finding Invasive Species

Scientists work hard to get rid of invasive species. However, finding them can be difficult. Citizen scientists can help. They can collect data about the invasive species in the areas where they live.

Finding invasive species early is important. Only a small number may be present in an area at first. That makes it easier to stop their spread. Citizen scientists may also notice new invasive species before scientists do. This is because there are many citizen scientists. They can **monitor** lots of different areas.

Citizen scientist data also helps scientists monitor known invasive species. Scientists can check if their removal projects are working. They can see if a species is spreading. And they can decide which areas need more help.

Collecting Data

Citizen scientists can report invasive species in many ways. The website iNaturalist is one place to do it. It records sightings of species from around the world. Citizen scientists can record any invasive species they spot. They can say where they saw the species. They can add a picture of it.

People can also use the Early Detection and Distribution Mapping System (EDDMapS).

Kudzu is a common invasive plant in the southeastern United States.

Citizen scientists can take photos of species they find.

This website is run by the University of Georgia. Citizen scientists record where they saw invasive species. They can also add pictures. More than 8.7 million sightings have been recorded on EDDMapS.

Zebra Mussels

Zebra mussels are a common invasive species. They are tiny animals with shells. Zebra mussels are native to Europe and Asia. In the 1980s, they spread to North America. Now they live in many North American lakes.

Zebra mussels take food from native species. They also attach themselves to native **mollusks**.

Finding Zebra Mussels

Some citizen scientists search for invasive species. This work is called surveying. People can survey public lakes for zebra mussels. Citizen scientists should check boat launches and beaches. They should take pictures of any zebra mussels they find. They should write down the time and place. Then they can report the data.

Each zebra mussel is about the size of a fingernail.

That kills the native mollusks. Zebra mussels can even get into underwater machines, including the motors of boats, and break them.

Zebra mussels spread very quickly. This means citizen scientists should report sightings right away. People can report zebra mussels on EDDMapS. In the United States, people can also use the US Geological Survey website. Some areas even have phone numbers for reporting.

Primary Source

Scientist Lindsay Chadderton explains how invasive species can harm environments:

> Invasive species tend to be aggressive, reproduce quickly and have few, if any, natural predators. As a result, they are able to quickly spread and **outcompete** native [species] for food and habitat.

Source: "Aquatic Invasive Species Management." *Nature Conservancy*, n.d., nature.org. Accessed 30 Apr. 2025.

Comparing Texts

Think about the quote. Does it support the information in this chapter? Or does it give a different perspective? Explain how in two to three sentences.

Purple loosestrife can grow in shallow water. It may also grow on land near water.

CHAPTER 3

Protecting the Planet

Not all invasive species projects focus on reporting species. Some projects work to remove invasive species. One such project attempts to remove purple loosestrife. Purple loosestrife is a flowering plant. It is native to Europe and Asia.

People brought the plant to North America in the 1800s. Now it grows throughout the United States and Canada. It is found in areas with lots of water.

Purple loosestrife spreads very fast. A single purple loosestrife plant can make more than 2 million seeds each year. Many of those seeds grow into full plants.

Preventing the Spread

Many invasive species are difficult to remove once they have arrived. The best way to fight the spread is to stop their entry. People should clean boats and paddles. That can prevent invasive fish and mussel species from spreading. People can also clean their hiking boots. That keeps plant species from spreading.

Orange daylily is invasive in North America. Gardeners should dig the plant, including the roots, out of their gardens.

In some areas, invasive purple loosestrife takes over. Native plants may not have room to grow. The spread can destroy habitats where native animals live too.

Citizen Scientists to the Rescue

Citizen scientists can help fight purple loosestrife. In public areas, people can pull up the plants. After that, people dry out the plants. That stops their seeds from spreading into bodies of water.

People can use beetles against purple loosestrife too. *Galerucella* beetles eat only purple loosestrife plants. So some areas have started programs to raise these beetles.

Galerucella beetles can remove all of the leaves from a plant. That makes it harder for the plant to grow.

The programs give the beetles out to citizen scientists.

The volunteers raise the beetles for a few months. Then they release the beetles. They put the bugs into areas with purple loosestrife.

Citizen scientists should wear gloves for safety when fighting invasive species.

The beetles can help destroy the purple loosestrife. The rest of the environment is not hurt.

Citizen scientists play big roles in the fight against invasive species. In some projects, they help scientists collect data about known invasive species. In others, helpers spot new invasive species. And citizen scientists can even help remove invasive species from their areas. These actions keep the planet healthy.

Explore Online

Look at the website below. Does it give any new information about invasive plants?

Invasive Plants

abdocorelibrary.com/invasive-species-projects

Science Projects

Citizen scientists recording invasive species that they see need access to project websites.

Volunteers collecting eDNA need special equipment and a place to send their samples.

Volunteers removing invasive plants must be familiar with the invasive plants in their area and know local rules about removing plants.

Citizen scientists raising *Galerucella* beetles to eat purple loosestrife need places to raise and release the beetles.

Glossary

data
information

ecosystem
a community of living and nonliving things that interact with each other

genetic material
the building blocks that make up living things

mollusks
a type of animal with a shell, such as snails and mussels

monitor
to watch or keep track of

outcompete
to take the things another species needs, causing them to not have enough

species
a group of similar living things that can produce young with one another

Online Resources

To learn more about invasive species projects, visit our free resource websites below.

Visit **abdocorelibrary.com** or scan this QR code for free Common Core resources for teachers and students, including vetted activities, multimedia, and booklinks, for deeper subject comprehension.

Visit **abdobooklinks.com** or scan this QR code for free additional online weblinks for further learning. These links are routinely monitored and updated to provide the most current information available.

Learn More

Kaner, Etta. *Beware the Burmese Pythons and Other Invasive Animal Species.* Kids Can, 2022.

Smith, Roland. *They Are Here! How Invasive Species Are Spoiling Our Ecosystems.* Godwin, 2023.

Index

About the Author

Christa Kelly is an author and editor from Minnesota. She lives with her wife and their two cats, Casey and Honey Cheddar.